brownies

brownies

Linda Collister photography by Richard Jung

RYLAND
PETERS
& SMALL

LONDON NEW YORK

First published in the
United States in 2006
by Ryland Peters & Small, Inc.
519 Broadway, 5th Floor
New York, NY 10012
www.rylandpeters.com

10 9 8 7 6 5 4 3 2

Library of Congress Cataloging-in-
Publication Data

Collister, Linda.
  Brownies / Linda Collister ;
photography by Richard Jung.
       p. cm.
  Includes index.
  ISBN-13: 978-1-84597-210-3
  ISBN-10: 1-84597-210-4
  1. Brownies (Cookery) I. Title.
  TX771.C557 2006
  641.8'653--dc22

2006008386

Notes
• All spoon measurements are level
unless otherwise specified.
• Ovens should be preheated to the
specified temperatures. All ovens work
slightly differently. I recommend using
an oven thermometer and suggest you
consult the maker's handbook for any
special instructions—particularly if you
are using a fan-assisted oven as you
may need to adjust cooking temperatures
according to manufacturer's instructions.

Senior Designer Steve Painter
Commissioning Editor Julia Charles
Production Controller Eleanor Cant
Art Director Anne-Marie Bulat
Publishing Director Alison Starling
Food Stylist Linda Tubby
Props Stylist Roísín Nield
Index Hilary Bird

Author's acknowledgments
I would like to thank the many people
who helped with this book; Barbara Levy,
Steve Painter, Julia Charles, Richard Jung,
Linda Tubby, and Roísín Nield.

contents

introduction

Brownies are both unpretentious and decadent. They are quick and easy to put together, yet immensely rich and satisfying. So what makes a chocolate brownie different from cake? The texture is crucial. A good brownie should be soft, with a close, moist, fudgy quality completely unlike the crumbly, open, and light texture of a pound cake. For this reason it is always far better to undercook brownies slightly, than to overcook them.

It's well worth using the best quality chocolate you can find—choose bars made with around 70 per cent cocoa solids which will give a good depth of flavor. Cocoa powder is also often added to increase the intensity of flavor without adding more sugar. The same applies to white chocolate—use very good quality, not children's bars, for a deep flavor rather than a cloying sweetness.

I've included old-fashioned brownies plus some new ones that may shock the purists! Although the "classic" brownies use pecans or walnuts, many of these recipes are nut-free. Some are "grown-up" brownies with a dash of Kirsch or rum, some are muffins for lunchboxes and, because I like to serve brownies at the end of a meal, I've included some delicious desserts, as well as sauces. But, all you really need is a glass of cold milk or a hot cup of coffee, and a square of brownie, warm from the oven.

making a classic brownie

If you've never made brownies before, this easy recipe for a Classic Fudge Brownie will get you hooked. It's the first one I ever made and it's a winner! Eat it warm from the oven with a scoop of vanilla ice cream and Chocolate Fudge Sauce (see page 61).

3½ oz. good bittersweet chocolate,

9 tablespoons unsalted butter

1½ cups superfine sugar

1 teaspoon real vanilla extract

2 extra-large eggs

⅔ cup all-purpose flour

2 tablespoons unsweetened cocoa powder

1 cup pecan halves or pieces

1¾ oz. good bittersweet chocolate, roughly chopped or choc chips

a brownie pan, 8 x 10 inches, greased and base-lined

Makes 20

Preheat the oven to 350°F. Break the 3½ oz. chocolate into pieces and put it in a heatproof bowl. Set the bowl over a saucepan of steaming water and melt the chocolate gently, stirring frequently. Remove the bowl from the saucepan and leave to cool until needed.

Put the butter in a large mixing bowl and, using either a wooden spoon or an electric mixer, beat until soft and creamy. Add the sugar and vanilla and continue beating until the mixture is soft and fluffy. Gradually beat in the eggs then beat in the melted chocolate.

Sift the flour and cocoa onto the mixture and stir in. When thoroughly combined add the nuts and the chocolate pieces (or choc chips) and stir in. Transfer the mixture to the prepared pan and spread evenly.

Bake in the preheated oven for about 25 to 30 minutes until a skewer inserted halfway between the sides and the center comes out just clean. Remove the pan from the oven. Leave to cool until just warm before removing from the pan and cutting into 20 pieces. Best eaten warm. Once cold, store in an airtight container and eat within 5 days.

brownies

Some brownie enthusiasts believe that only cocoa should be used, not melted chocolate, as it gives a deeper, truly intense chocolate flavor which balances the sugar necessary to give a brownie the required fudgy texture.

old-fashioned brownies

1 cup walnut pieces

4 extra-large eggs

1½ cups superfine sugar

1¼ sticks butter, melted

½ teaspoon real vanilla extract

1 cup plus 2 tablespoons all-purpose flour

¾ cup unsweetened cocoa powder

a brownie pan, 20.5 x 25.5 cm, greased and base-lined

Makes 16

Preheat the oven to 325°F. Put the walnut pieces in an ovenproof dish and lightly toast in the oven for about 10 minutes. Leave to cool. Don't turn off the oven.

Meanwhile break the eggs into a mixing bowl. Use an electric mixer to whisk until frothy then whisk in the sugar. Whisk for a minute then, still whisking constantly, add the melted butter in a steady stream. Whisk for a minute more, then whisk in the vanilla.

Sieve the flour and cocoa into the bowl and stir in using a wooden spoon. When thoroughly combined stir in the nuts. Transfer the mixture to the prepared pan and spread evenly.

Bake in the preheated oven for about 25 minutes until a skewer inserted halfway between the sides and the center comes out just clean. Remove the pan from the oven.

Leave to cool completely before removing from the pan and cutting into 16 pieces. Store in an airtight container and eat within 5 days.

There's a lot of chocolate in this recipe, but it's not too sweet due to the cocoa content and the addition of either walnut or pecan pieces. These brownies are particularly good eaten warm with whipped cream.

very rich brownies

7 oz. good bittersweet chocolate

7 tablespoons butter, softened

1½ cups firm-packed soft light brown sugar

4 extra-large eggs, lightly beaten

½ teaspoon real vanilla extract

½ cup all-purpose flour

⅔ cup unsweetened cocoa powder

1 cup walnut or pecan pieces

chocolate shavings, to decorate

a brownie pan, 8 x 10 inches, greased and base-lined

Makes 20

Preheat the oven to 350°F. Break up the chocolate and put it in a heatproof bowl. Set the bowl over a saucepan of steaming water and gently melt the chocolate, stirring frequently. Remove the bowl from the saucepan and leave to cool until needed.

Put the butter and sugar into a mixing bowl and, using either a wooden spoon or an electric mixer, beat until fluffy. Gradually beat in the eggs then the vanilla. Next, beat in the melted chocolate. When thoroughly combined sift the flour and cocoa onto the mixture and stir in. Mix in the nuts then transfer to the prepared pan and spread evenly.

Bake in the preheated oven for about 20 minutes or until almost firm to the touch. Remove the pan from the oven.

Leave to cool before removing from the pan and cutting into 20 pieces. Sprinkle with chocolate shavings before serving. (These are made by grating bittersweet chocolate on the coarse hole side of a grater.) Store in an airtight container and eat within 4 days.

Black cherries, Kirsch, and rich, bittersweet chocolate are a classic combination. Here, pitted black cherries preserved in a Kirsch syrup are dropped into a well-flavored, not too sweet, double-chocolate brownie mixture. It makes a perfect dessert for a New Year's party, when fruits preserved in alcohol are readily available from stores. For an alcohol-free alternative use black cherries canned in either juice or a light syrup. Delicious served with Crème Chantilly (see page 44).

black forest brownies

8 oz. good bittersweet chocolate

9 tablespoons butter

3 tablespoons heavy cream

3 extra-large eggs

1 cup plus 3 tablespoons superfine sugar

2 tablespoons Kirsch or Kirsch syrup from a jar (optional)

1⅓ cups all-purpose flour

3½ oz. good bittersweet chocolate, roughly chopped or ⅔ cup choc chips

1 x 16-oz. can black cherries (6 oz. drained weight)

confectioners' sugar, for dusting

a brownie pan, 8 x 10 inches, greased and base-lined

Makes 24

Preheat the oven to 350°F. Break up the 8 oz. chocolate and put it in a heatproof bowl. Add the butter and cream to the bowl and set it over a saucepan of steaming water. Melt gently, stirring frequently. Remove the bowl from the saucepan and leave to cool until needed.

Break the eggs into the bowl of an electric mixer and whisk just until frothy. Add the sugar and Kirsch (if using) and whisk until thick and mousse-like. Whisk in the melted chocolate mixture.

Sift the flour onto the mixture and stir in. When thoroughly combined stir in the pieces of chocolate. Transfer the mixture to the prepared pan and spread evenly. Gently drop the cherries onto the brownie mixture, spacing them as evenly as possible.

Bake in the preheated oven for 30 to 35 minutes until a skewer inserted halfway between the sides and the center comes out just clean. Remove the pan from the oven.

Leave until cool before carefully removing from the pan and cutting into 24 pieces. Serve dusted with confectioners' sugar. Store in an airtight container and eat within 4 days.

Walnuts have a creamy, bittersweet taste that contrasts well with the sweetness of the brownie mixture. Here, there is a high proportion of walnuts to mixture, plus a fudgy walnut frosting. For a deeper flavor toast the nuts for 10 minutes in the oven before adding to both the brownie and frosting mixtures.

extra-nutty brownies

3½ oz. good bittersweet chocolate

1 stick unsalted butter

1¼ cups firm-packed soft light brown sugar

½ teaspoon real vanilla extract

2 extra-large eggs, lightly beaten

¾ cup all-purpose flour

2 tablespoons unsweetened cocoa powder

1½ cups walnut pieces

Frosting:

2 oz. good bittersweet chocolate

½ stick unsalted butter

2 tablespoons milk (not fat-free)

2 tablespoons unsweetened cocoa powder

¾ cup firm-packed confectioners' sugar

½ cup walnut pieces

a brownie pan, 8 x 10 inches, greased and base-lined

Makes 20

Preheat the oven to 350°F. Break up the chocolate and put it in a heatproof mixing bowl with the butter. Set the bowl over a saucepan of steaming water and melt gently, stirring frequently.

Remove the bowl from the saucepan and stir in the sugar and vanilla. Add the eggs and beat well with a wooden spoon until the mixture comes together as a smooth batter.

Sift the flour and cocoa into the bowl and stir in. When thoroughly combined stir in the nuts. Transfer the mixture to the prepared pan and spread evenly.

Bake in the preheated oven for about 15 minutes or until just firm to the touch. Remove the pan from the oven. Leave to cool completely then carefully remove the brownie from the pan.

Meanwhile make the frosting: melt the chocolate and butter as above. Remove the bowl from the saucepan and stir in the milk.

Sift the cocoa and confectioners' sugar into the bowl and stir in. When thick and smooth, stir in the nuts. Spread the frosting over the cooled, baked brownie.

Once the frosting is firm, cut the brownie into 20 pieces. Store in an airtight container and eat within 4 days.

The sharpness of dried cranberries balances the sweetness of this bittersweet chocolate brownie, and the tangy grated orange zest lifts the richness.

cranberry and bittersweet chocolate brownies

7 oz. good bittersweet chocolate

1¾ sticks unsalted butter, diced

3 extra-large eggs

1 cup less 1 tablespoon of superfine sugar

grated zest of 1 medium unwaxed orange

1½ cups all-purpose flour

⅔ cup dried cranberries

a brownie pan, 8 x 10 inches, greased and base-lined

Makes 20

Preheat the oven to 350°F. Break up the chocolate and put it in a heatproof mixing bowl with the butter. Set the bowl over a saucepan of steaming water and melt gently, stirring frequently. Remove the bowl from the saucepan and leave to cool.

Whisk the eggs until frothy using an electric mixer or whisk. Add the sugar and orange zest and whisk until the mixture becomes very thick and mousse-like. Whisk in the melted chocolate mixture.

Sift the flour onto the mixture and stir in. When everything is thoroughly combined stir in the dried cranberries. Transfer the mixture to the prepared pan and spread evenly.

Bake in the preheated oven for about 25 minutes or until a skewer inserted halfway between the sides and the center comes out just clean. Remove the pan from the oven.

Leave to cool before removing from the pan and cutting into 20 pieces. Store in an airtight container and eat within 5 days.

Ginger with chocolate is a delicious taste sensation. Here good bittersweet chocolate flavored with pieces of candied ginger is used in a chocolate brownie mixture. Just a hint of spice, plus deliciously tangy soured cream, makes these brownies extra special.

soured cream and spice brownies

7 oz. good bittersweet chocolate

7 tablespoons unsalted butter

4 extra-large eggs

1 cup superfine or granulated sugar

¾ cup all-purpose flour

¼ teaspoon ground cinnamon

½ teaspoon ground ginger

3 tablespoons soured cream

2 oz. bittersweet chocolate with candied ginger pieces, chopped

a brownie pan, 8 x 10 inches, greased and base-lined

Makes 20

Preheat the oven to 350°F. Break up the 7 oz. bittersweet chocolate and put it in a heatproof mixing bowl with the butter. Set the bowl over a saucepan of steaming water and melt gently, stirring frequently. Remove the bowl from the saucepan and leave to cool until needed.

Put the eggs and sugar into the bowl of an electric mixer and whisk until very thick and mousse-like. Whisk in the melted chocolate mixture.

Sift the flour and spices into the bowl and stir in. Mix in the soured cream followed by the chopped chocolate with ginger. Transfer to the prepared pan and spread evenly.

Bake in the preheated oven for about 25 minutes or until a skewer inserted halfway between the sides and the center comes out just clean. Remove the pan from the oven.

Leave to cool before carefully removing from the pan and cutting into 20 pieces. Store in an airtight container and eat within 5 days.

This brownie is rich and fudgy with masses of chocolate, plus a good shot of strong espresso coffee to offset the sweetness. Serve with a little light cream and you have an elegant dessert.

espresso brownies

8 oz. good bittersweet chocolate

1 stick unsalted butter, softened

1½ cups superfine or granulated sugar

5 extra-large eggs, lightly beaten

4 tablespoons strong espresso coffee, room temperature

½ cup plus 1 tablespoon all-purpose flour

¾ cup unsweetened cocoa powder, plus extra for dusting

a brownie pan, 8 x 10 inches, greased and base-lined

Makes 20

Preheat the oven to 350°F. Break up the chocolate and put it in a heatproof bowl. Set the bowl over a saucepan of steaming water and melt gently, stirring frequently. Remove the bowl from the saucepan and leave to cool until needed.

Put the soft butter and sugar into the bowl of an electric mixer and beat until light and fluffy. Alternatively, you can also use a mixing bowl and wooden spoon. Gradually beat in the eggs, then the coffee.

Sift the flour and cocoa into the bowl and stir in. Add the cooled melted chocolate and mix in. When thoroughly combined transfer the mixture to the prepared pan and spread evenly.

Bake in the preheated oven for about 25 minutes or until a skewer inserted halfway between the sides and the center comes out just clean. Remove the pan from the oven.

Leave to cool for 10 minutes before lightly dusting with cocoa powder, removing from the pan and cutting into 20 pieces. Serve warm or at room temperature. Once cool, store in an airtight container and eat within 5 days.

A simple all-in-one recipe that owes its lovely, intense flavor to bittersweet chocolate flavored with strong coffee. This chocolate is most often sold in bars labeled as "espresso chocolate."

easy mocha brownies

3½ oz. good bittersweet espresso-flavored chocolate

1½ sticks unsalted butter, diced

1 cup plus 3 tablespoons superfine or granulated sugar

3 extra-large eggs, lightly beaten

⅓ cup plus 1 tablespoon all-purpose flour

1½ cups walnut pieces

a brownie pan, 8 x 8 inches, greased and base-lined

Makes 9

Preheat the oven to 350°F. Break up the chocolate and put it in a heatproof mixing bowl with the butter. Set the bowl over a saucepan of steaming water and leave to melt gently, stirring very frequently.

Remove the bowl from the saucepan and stir in the sugar. Stir in the beaten eggs. When thoroughly combined stir in the flour, then finally mix in the nuts. Transfer the mixture to the prepared pan and spread evenly.

Bake in the preheated oven for about 25 to 30 minutes or until a skewer inserted halfway between the sides and the center comes out just clean. Remove the pan from the oven.

Leave to cool before removing from the pan and cutting into 9 large pieces. Store in an airtight container and eat within 5 days.

These to-die-for brownies are incredibly rich in chocolate yet not too sweet. This is a very useful recipe when you need a flour-free dessert or cake. Under-cooking is vital to avoid a dry brownie.

flourless-yet-fudgy brownies

10 oz. good bittersweet chocolate

1⅓ sticks unsalted butter, diced

½ cup unsweetened cocoa powder, sifted

4 extra-large eggs

1 cup superfine or granulated sugar

1 cup walnut or pecan pieces

confectioners' sugar, for dusting

a brownie pan, 8 x 10 inches, greased and base-lined

Makes 12

Preheat the oven to 350°F. Break up the chocolate and put it in a heatproof bowl with the butter. Set the bowl over a saucepan of steaming hot water and melt gently, stirring frequently. Remove the bowl from the saucepan and stir in the cocoa. Set aside.

Put the eggs into a mixing bowl and beat well with a whisk or electric mixer. Add the sugar and whisk thoroughly until very light and frothy and doubled in volume.

Using a large metal spoon, carefully fold in the chocolate mixture followed by the nuts. Transfer the mixture to the prepared pan and spread evenly.

Bake in the preheated oven for about 25 to 30 minutes until the top of the brownie is just firm to the touch but the center is still slightly soft.

Leave to cool for 10 minutes before carefully removing from the pan. Dust with confectioners' sugar before cutting into 12 pieces. Serve warm or at room temperature with soured cream or crème fraîche. Once cool, store in an airtight container and eat within 4 days.

peanut butter brownies

Chocolate and peanuts is a classic combination. This recipe is included by popular demand from my American family. I always use a top-quality peanut butter with no added sugar or oil as it gives the best flavor.

3½ oz. good bittersweet chocolate

1½ sticks unsalted butter, diced

3 extra-large eggs

1¼ cups firm-packed soft light brown sugar

1 cup less 1 tablespoon all-purpose flour

2 tablespoons unsweetened cocoa powder

Peanut mixture:

¾ cup smooth peanut butter

¼ cup superfine or granulated sugar

1 tablespoon all-purpose flour

5 tablespoons milk (not fat-free)

2 tablespoons roasted, unsalted peanuts

a brownie pan, 8 x 10 inches, greased and base-lined

Makes 16

Preheat the oven to 350°F. Break up the chocolate and put it in a heatproof bowl with the butter. Set the bowl over a saucepan of steaming hot water and melt gently, stirring frequently. Remove the bowl from the saucepan and leave to cool until needed.

Break the eggs into a mixing bowl and beat well with a whisk or an electric mixer. Add the sugar and whisk until the mixture is very thick and mousse-like.

Whisk in the melted chocolate mixture. Sift the flour and cocoa onto the mixture and mix until thoroughly combined. Transfer the mixture to the prepared pan and spread evenly.

Put all the ingredients for the peanut mixture into a bowl and mix well. Drop teaspoonfuls of the mixture, evenly spaced, onto the chocolate mixture. Use the end of a chopstick or teaspoon handle to marble or swirl both mixtures. Scatter the peanuts over the top.

Bake in the preheated oven for about 30 minutes or until just firm. Leave to cool before removing from the pan and cutting into 16 pieces. Store in an airtight container and eat within 5 days.

This recipe is for my husband, who came across these unusual brownies in a San Francisco deli and begged me to make them for him at home. You'll need a box (or bar) of bittersweet chocolate with a soft, mint-flavored fondant center—of the type that is most often sold as "after-dinner" mints.

mint brownies

4½ oz. good bittersweet chocolate

7 tablespoons unsalted butter

3 extra-large eggs

1 cup superfine or granulated sugar

¾ cup all-purpose flour

2 tablespoons unsweetened cocoa powder

3½ oz.–7 oz. bittersweet chocolate with mint center (depending on strength of flavor required)

a brownie pan, 8 x 10 inches, greased

Makes 20

Preheat the oven to 350°F. Break up the bittersweet chocolate and put it in a heatproof bowl with the butter. Set the bowl over a saucepan of steaming water and melt gently, stirring frequently. Remove the bowl from the saucepan and set aside to cool.

Whisk the eggs using an electric mixer or whisk then add the sugar and whisk until thick and mousse-like.

Whisk in the melted chocolate mixture. Sift the flour and cocoa onto the mixture and stir in. When thoroughly combined spoon half the brownie mixture into the prepared pan and spread evenly.

Leave the mint chocolates whole or break them up (depending on the size of the ones you are using). Arrange them over the brownie mixture already in the pan. Spoon the remaining brownie mixture on top and gently spread to cover the chocolate mints.

Bake in the preheated oven for about 25 minutes or until a skewer inserted halfway between the sides and the center comes out just clean (though some of the sticky mint layer will appear). Remove the pan from the oven.

Leave to cool before removing from the pan and cutting into 20 pieces. Store in an airtight container and eat within 5 days.

These dark, double-chocolate brownies have a light texture and are subtly flavored with rum. Serve them with vanilla ice cream for a perfect dessert.

choc choc rum brownies

2 oz. good bittersweet chocolate

6 tablespoons unsalted butter

1½ cups firm-packed confectioners' sugar

2 extra-large eggs, lightly beaten

2 tablespoons dark rum

½ cup all-purpose flour

3½ oz. good bittersweet chocolate, finely chopped or ⅔ cup choc chips

½ cup walnut pieces

a brownie pan, 8 x 10 inches, greased and base-lined

Makes 16

Preheat the oven to 350°F. Break up the 2 oz. bittersweet chocolate and put it in a heatproof bowl. Set the bowl over a saucepan of steaming water and melt gently, stirring frequently. Remove the bowl from the saucepan and leave to cool.

Put the softened butter and confectioners' sugar into the bowl of an electric mixer and beat until light and creamy, using slow speed at first. Alternatively, use a mixing bowl and wooden spoon.

Gradually beat in the eggs, followed by the rum. Scrape down the sides then beat in the melted chocolate. Stir in the flour, and when thoroughly combined, add the chopped chocolate or the choc chips and the nuts and mix thoroughly. Transfer the mixture to the prepared pan and spread evenly.

Bake in the preheated oven for about 20 to 25 minutes until the top is set and firm. Leave to cool before removing from the pan—taking care as the crust is fragile—and cutting into 16 pieces.

Serve warm or at room temperature. Once cool, store in an airtight container and eat within 4 days.

brownie "muffins"

My children asked for a brownie that could survive life in a
school lunchbox. It needed to be nut-free, not too big and,
most importantly, not fall apart. I came up with this delicious
brownie-style muffin packed with choc chips and baked in
a paper case. The perfect solution!

2 extra-large eggs

¾ cup firm-packed soft light brown sugar

9 tablespoons unsalted butter, melted

1 cup milk (not fat-free)

½ teaspoon real vanilla extract

1⅔ cups all-purpose flour

½ cup unsweetened cocoa powder

½ teaspoon baking powder

2 tablespoons white choc chips

2 tablespoons bittersweet or semisweet choc chips, plus extra to decorate

a 12-cup muffin pan, lined with 12 paper cases

Makes 12

Preheat the oven to 350°F. Break the eggs into a mixing bowl, add the sugar and beat with a wooden spoon until thoroughly combined. Beat in the melted butter, followed by the milk and the vanilla.

Sift the flour, cocoa, and baking powder onto the mixture and mix in. Finally, stir in the choc chips. Divide the mixture equally between the paper cases and sprinkle a few extra choc chips on the top of each muffin to decorate.

Bake in the preheated oven for about 20 to 25 minutes until just firm to the touch. The brownies will only rise slightly and won't resemble peaked muffins.

Remove the pan from the oven then remove the muffins from the pan and allow them to cool on a wire cooling tray. Store in an airtight container and eat within 5 days.

blondies

This Australian recipe is packed with rich, buttery macadamia nuts. For the best flavor use nuts from an unopened pack as they spoil quickly.

macadamia and white chocolate blondies

6 oz. good white chocolate, chopped

1 stick unsalted butter, diced

½ cup superfine or granulated sugar

2 extra-large eggs, lightly beaten

½ teaspoon real vanilla extract

1 cup all-purpose flour

½ teaspoon baking powder

1¼ cups macadamia nuts, roughly chopped

3½ oz. good bittersweet or white chocolate, roughly chopped or ⅔ cup choc chips

a brownie pan, 8 x 10 inches, greased and base-lined

Makes 20

Preheat the oven to 350°F. Put the 6 oz. of chopped white chocolate and the diced butter into a heatproof mixing bowl, then set over a saucepan of steaming water. Melt gently, stirring frequently.

Remove the bowl from the pan and stir in the sugar with a wooden spoon—don't worry if the mixture looks curdled. Gradually stir in the beaten eggs, then the vanilla, and beat for a minute until the mixture becomes thick, smooth, and glossy.

Sift the flour and baking powder onto the mixture and stir in. When thoroughly combined stir in two-thirds of the chopped nuts, and the chopped chocolate or choc chips.

Transfer the mixture to the prepared pan and spread evenly. Scatter the remaining nuts over the top.

Bake in the preheated oven for about 20 to 25 minutes or until golden brown and a skewer inserted halfway between the sides and the center comes out just clean.

Leave to cool before removing from the pan and cutting into 20 pieces. Store in an airtight container and eat within 4 days.

This lovely blondie, made with the best white chocolate and fresh raspberries, makes a heavenly summer dessert. It is rich but not too heavy. Serve with a fresh raspberry sauce and vanilla ice cream.

white chocolate and raspberry blondies

9 oz. good white chocolate

1¾ sticks unsalted butter, diced

3 extra-large eggs

¾ cup superfine or granulated sugar

½ teaspoon real vanilla extract

1½ cups all-purpose flour

1 teaspoon baking powder

1½ cups fresh raspberries

a brownie pan, 8 x 8 inches, greased and base-lined

Makes 9

Preheat the oven to 350°F. Break up 5 oz. of the chocolate and put it in a heatproof mixing bowl with the butter. Set the bowl over a saucepan of steaming water. Melt gently, stirring frequently. Remove the bowl from the saucepan and leave to cool until needed.

Break the eggs into the bowl of an electric mixer or a mixing bowl. Whisk until frothy then add the sugar and the vanilla and beat thoroughly until very thick and mousse-like.

Whisk in the melted chocolate mixture. Sift the flour and baking powder onto the mixture and fold in. Chop the rest of the chocolate into pieces the size of the nail on your pinkie and stir them in. Spoon the mixture into the prepared pan and spread evenly. Scatter the fresh raspberries over the top.

Bake in the preheated oven for about 25 minutes or until a skewer inserted halfway between the sides and the center comes out just clean. Leave to cool before removing from the pan and cutting into 9 large pieces. Store in an airtight container and eat within 2 days.

coconut blondies

Slightly sticky and very chewy, these delicious blondies are
heavy with coconut, as well as bittersweet and white chocolate.
You will need to use the unsweetened type of dried and shredded
packaged coconut.

2 cups unsweetened "desiccated" shredded coconut

1½ sticks unsalted butter

2 cups firm-packed light brown sugar

2 extra-large eggs, lightly beaten

1 teaspoon real vanilla extract

1½ cups all-purpose flour

1 teaspoon baking powder

⅓ cup bittersweet choc chips

⅓ cup white choc chips

a brownie pan, 8 x 10 inches, greased and base-lined

Makes 20

Preheat the oven to 350°F. Put the coconut into a heatproof baking dish and toast in the preheated oven for about 5 minutes, stirring frequently, until a light golden brown. Remove from the oven and set aside to cool. Leave the oven on.

Melt the butter in a medium-sized saucepan over low heat. Remove the saucepan from the heat and stir in the sugar with a wooden spoon.

Gradually beat in the eggs then the vanilla. Sift the flour and baking powder onto the mixture and stir in. Finally, work in the coconut and both the bittersweet and white choc chips.

When everything is thoroughly combined transfer the mixture to the prepared pan and spread evenly.

Bake in the preheated oven for about 20 to 25 minutes or until golden brown and a skewer inserted halfway between the sides and the center comes out just clean.

Leave to cool before removing from the pan and cutting into 20 pieces. Store in an airtight container and eat within 5 days.

This blondie doesn't contain any nuts but if you want to add some, simply replace the bittersweet chocolate with 4 oz. walnut halves.

butterscotch blondies

1 stick unsalted butter

1⅓ cups lightly-packed soft light brown sugar

2 extra-large eggs, lightly beaten

½ teaspoon real vanilla extract

1⅓ cups all-purpose flour

½ teaspoon baking powder

3½ oz. good bittersweet chocolate, chopped or ⅔ cup choc chips

a brownie pan, 8 x 10 inches, greased and base-lined

Makes 20

Preheat the oven to 350°F. Put the butter in a medium-sized saucepan and melt gently over low heat.

Remove the saucepan from the heat and stir in the sugar with a wooden spoon. Gradually stir in the eggs then the vanilla and beat for a minute.

Sift the flour and baking powder onto the mixture and stir in. Add the chocolate pieces or choc chips (or walnuts if using) and stir until thoroughly combined. Transfer the mixture to the prepared pan and spread evenly.

Bake in the preheated oven for about 25 minutes until light golden brown and a skewer inserted halfway between the sides and the center comes out just clean.

Leave to cool before removing from the pan and cutting into 20 pieces. Store in an airtight container and eat within 5 days.

Crème Chantilly: To make this light and slightly sweetened whipped cream, first chill a whisk and mixing bowl for an hour in the fridge or freezer. Put 1 cup whipping cream, well chilled, into the bowl. Whisk until thickened. Add ½ teaspoon of real vanilla extract and 1½ tablespoons of superfine sugar. Whisk again until the cream is very thick and forms soft peaks. Stop at this point to avoid overwhipping then pile the cream into a bowl and serve immediately or cover and chill for up to 2 hours.

This is a deliciously moist and chewy little blondie packed with pecan halves, rather than pieces.

cinnamon pecan blondies

7 tablespoons unsalted butter

2 cups soft light brown sugar

½ teaspoon ground cinnamon

2 extra-large eggs, lightly beaten

1 cup plus 2 tablespoons all-purpose flour

1 teaspoon baking powder

1 cup pecan halves

a brownie pan, 8 x 10 inches, greased and base-lined

Makes 30

Preheat the oven to 350°F. Put the butter in a medium-sized saucepan. Set it over low heat and melt gently. Add the sugar and cinnamon and stir until smooth and melted. Remove the saucepan from the heat and leave to cool for a few minutes.

Use a wooden spoon to stir in the eggs, beating the mixture well until thoroughly combined. Sift the flour and baking powder onto the mixture, then stir in.

Mix in the pecans then transfer the mixture to the prepared pan and spread evenly.

Bake in the preheated oven for about 25 minutes until golden brown and a skewer inserted halfway between the sides and the center comes out just clean.

Leave to cool for 5 minutes then loosen and remove from the pan. Wait until it is completely cold before cutting into 30 pieces. Store in an airtight container and eat within 4 days.

Incredibly rich and very moreish! This recipe uses cream cheese instead of butter and then half the mixture is flavored with white chocolate, the rest with bittersweet chocolate. Walnuts are added at the end to give a contrast in taste and texture.

half blondie, half brownie

3½ oz. good bittersweet chocolate

2 oz. good white chocolate

10 oz. cream cheese

1 cup superfine or granulated sugar

3 extra-large eggs

1 teaspoon real vanilla extract

¾ cup all-purpose flour

1 cup walnut pieces

a brownie pan, 8 x 10 inches, greased and base-lined

Makes 30

Preheat the oven to 350°F. Break up the bittersweet chocolate and put it in a heatproof bowl. Set the bowl over a saucepan of steaming water and melt gently, stirring frequently. Remove the bowl from the saucepan and leave to cool until needed. Melt the white chocolate in the same way and leave to cool.

Put the cream cheese into the bowl of an electric mixer or food processor. Add the sugar and beat or process until smooth. Beat in the eggs, one at a time, then the vanilla. Work in the flour on low speed or using the "pulse" button.

Transfer half the mixture to another bowl. Add the melted bittersweet chocolate to one half and mix thoroughly. Mix the melted white chocolate into the other half. The bittersweet chocolate mixture will be stiffer than the white.

Using a tablespoon, drop spoonfuls of the bittersweet chocolate mixture into the prepared pan, spacing them evenly apart, with gaps between the blobs. Pour or spoon the white chocolate mixture over the top to fill the spaces. Scatter the nuts over the top. Use the end of a chopstick or the handle of a teaspoon to marble and swirl the two mixtures together.

Bake in the preheated oven for 25 to 30 minutes or until a skewer inserted halfway between the sides and the center comes out just clean.

Leave to cool before removing from the pan and cutting into 30 pieces. Store in an airtight container and eat within 5 days.

brownie desserts

This deliciously gooey brownie dessert is an ideal recipe for absolute beginners. If you have suitable oven to tableware it can be made, baked, and served in the same dish so it's a treat for chocolate lovers and dishwashers alike!

brownie lava dessert

½ cup pecan pieces

3½ oz. good bittersweet chocolate

1 stick unsalted butter, diced

1 cup less one tablespoon superfine or granulated sugar

2 extra-large eggs, lightly beaten

½ teaspoon real vanilla extract

½ cup all-purpose flour

a flameproof, ovenproof pie dish, approximately 7 inches (across top) and 2½ inches deep

Serves 4 to 6

Preheat the oven to 350°F. Put the pecan pieces into an ovenproof dish and lightly toast in the preheated oven for about 10 minutes. Remove from the oven and leave to cool.

Meanwhile break up the chocolate and put it in the pie dish (or in a medium-sized saucepan). Add the butter and melt gently over very, very low heat, stirring frequently.

Remove from the heat and stir in the sugar, then gradually stir in the eggs followed by the vanilla.

When thoroughly mixed, stir in the flour, then finally the nuts. When there are no floury streaks scrape down the sides of the dish (if this is what you are baking the dessert in) so the mixture doesn't scorch, and put it into the preheated oven or, if using a saucepan, transfer the mixture to a buttered soufflé dish or ovenproof dish.

Bake for about 30 minutes until the mixture is set on top with a soft gooey layer at the bottom.

Serve immediately with a pitcher of light cream for pouring, or vanilla ice cream.

Baking a brownie mixture in a crisp pastry shell means you can make a very soft, sticky, nutty brownie. This recipe is a family favorite and I always bake it as one of our Thanksgiving pies.

brownie fudge pie

Pastry:

1⅓ cups all-purpose flour

a pinch of salt

1 stick unsalted butter, chilled and diced

2–3 tablespoons iced water

Filling:

3 extra-large eggs

1 cup firm-packed soft light brown sugar

1 cup firm-packed soft dark brown sugar

½ teaspoon real vanilla extract

1½ sticks unsalted butter, melted

⅓ cup plus 1 tablespoon all-purpose flour

½ cup unsweetened cocoa powder

1½ cups pecan halves or pieces

a 9-inch loose-based pie or flan dish parchment paper pie weights

Serves 10

Preheat the oven to 350°F. To make the pastry in a food processor put the flour, salt, and diced butter in the bowl and process until the mixture resembles fine crumbs. With the machine running, add just enough water through the feed tube to make a slightly firm dough. Alternatively, to make the pastry by hand: put the flour, salt, and butter into a mixing bowl. Rub the pieces of butter into the flour with your fingertips until the mixture looks like fine crumbs. With a round-bladed knife stir in just enough water to bring the mixture together to make a slightly firm dough.

Wrap and chill for 15 minutes then roll out on a lightly-floured counter to a circle about 11 inches across and use to line the pie dish. Prick the base of the pastry shell all over with a fork then chill for 15 minutes. Line the pastry shell with parchment paper, fill with pie weights and bake "blind" in the preheated oven for 12 to 15 minutes until lightly golden and just firm. Carefully remove the paper and pie weights and bake for a further 5 minutes or until the shell is crisp and lightly golden. Remove from the oven and leave to cool.

Break the eggs into the bowl of an electric mixer. Whisk until frothy then add the sugar and whisk until very thick and mousse-like. Add the vanilla and whisk again to combine. Whisk in the melted butter. Remove the bowl from the mixer and sift the flour and cocoa onto the mixture. Fold in with a large metal spoon. When there are no streaks of flour left, gently stir in the pecans. Transfer the mixture into the pastry shell and spread evenly. Bake in the preheated oven for about 30 minutes or until firm to the touch. Remove from the oven.

Allow to cool slightly before removing from the dish. Serve warm with ice cream or Crème Chantilly (page 44). Store at room temperature in a covered container and eat within 5 days.

This special dessert is very easy to prepare using a food processor. The base is a thick, rich, brownie and the topping is a luxuriously deep chocolate cheesecake with pecans.

brownie cheesecake

Preheat the oven to 325°C. First make the base: put the pieces of butter, sugar, flour, and cocoa into the bowl of a food processor and process until the mixture becomes a thick paste.

Tip this mixture into the prepared pan and press onto the base to make a thick, even layer. Chill while making the topping.

Break up the chocolate and put it in a heatproof bowl. Set the bowl over a saucepan of steaming water and melt gently, stirring frequently. Remove the bowl from the saucepan and stir until smooth. Leave for 5 minutes to cool.

Put the cream cheese, eggs, sugar, and vanilla into the bowl of the food processor. Process until thoroughly combined, scraping down the sides from time to time.

With the machine running add the cream through the feed tube, followed by the melted chocolate. When completely mixed pour the mixture onto the base and spread evenly. Finish by scattering over the pecans.

Stand the pan on a baking sheet then bake in the preheated oven for 40 minutes until just firm. Turn off the oven but leave the cheesecake in the oven, without opening the door, to cool down. Then remove the cheesecake from the oven and chill at least 4 hours (preferably overnight) before removing from the pan.

Dust with cocoa before serving. Store in an airtight container in the fridge and eat within 5 days.

Base:

2 sticks plus 2 tablespoons unsalted butter, chilled and diced

1¼ cups superfine sugar

1½ cups all-purpose flour

½ cup unsweetened cocoa powder

Topping:

7 oz. good bittersweet chocolate

14 oz. cream cheese

2 extra-large eggs

⅓ cup superfine sugar

½ teaspoon real vanilla extract

1 cup heavy cream

½ cup pecan halves

unsweetened cocoa powder, for dusting

a 9-inch, round, springform baking pan, greased

Serves 12

My son recently asked for this as his birthday cake, along with a large pitcher of Creamy Chocolate Sauce. Here an easy all-in-one brownie mixture is made thinner and more pliable than usual, then sliced up and sandwiched with vanilla ice cream. Note that it must be frozen for at least six hours before serving.

brownie ice cream cake

7 oz. good bittersweet chocolate

5 tablespoons unsalted butter, diced

2 tablespoons water

¾ cup superfine or granulated sugar

2 extra-large eggs, lightly beaten

½ teaspoon real vanilla extract

¾ cup all-purpose flour

½ teaspoon baking powder

⅔ cup finely chopped toasted almonds

To assemble:

2 pints good quality vanilla ice cream

a jelly roll pan, 12 x 8 inches, greased and base-lined

Serves 8

Preheat the oven to 325°F. Break up the chocolate and put in a heatproof mixing bowl with the butter and water. Set the bowl over a saucepan of steaming water and melt gently, stirring frequently.

Add the sugar to the melted mixture and stir well to thoroughly combine. Remove the bowl from the saucepan and leave to cool for a couple of minutes.

Stir in the eggs and vanilla and mix well. Sift the flour and baking powder onto the mixture and mix in. Finally, stir in the nuts. Transfer the mixture to the prepared pan and spread evenly.

Bake in the preheated oven for about 15 to 20 minutes or until a skewer inserted in to the center of the mixture comes out just clean. Leave to cool completely before turning out onto a cutting board.

Cut the brownie in half lengthwise to make 2 long strips. Cut one of the strips into 8 equal pieces. Wrap the long strip and the 8 top pieces in foil and freeze until firm. When ready to assemble, transfer the ice cream to the fridge to slightly soften (it must not be allowed to melt). Put the long brownie strip onto a freezerproof serving platter or baking sheet, then pile the ice cream on top and quickly neaten the sides and top. Arrange the 8 brownie pieces on top. Return to the freezer until firm then wrap tightly and freeze for at least 6 hours before serving.

When ready to serve, use a sharp knife to cut into 8 portions and offer a pitcher of Creamy Chocolate Sauce (see page 62) for pouring. The assembled cake can be kept in the freezer for up to a week.

Here, a fudgy brownie made with plenty of chocolate and toasted pecans, and baked slightly thinner than usual, is combined with a good store-bought ice cream—either white chocolate or vanilla. Serve with your choice of hot sauce for pouring.

brownie ice cream

Brownie mix:

2 oz. good bittersweet chocolate

½ stick unsalted butter

⅔ cup light brown sugar

½ teaspoon real vanilla extract

1 extra-large egg, lightly beaten

⅓ cup plus 1 tablespoon all-purpose flour

1½ tablespoons unsweetened cocoa powder

¾ cup pecan pieces, toasted

To finish:

1¾ pints good white chocolate or vanilla ice cream

8-inch square baking pan, greased and base-lined a freezerproof container

Serves 6 to 8

Preheat the oven to 350°F. First make the brownie mix: break up the chocolate and put it in a heatproof bowl with the butter. Set the bowl over a saucepan of steaming water and melt gently, stirring frequently.

Remove the bowl from the saucepan and use a wooden spoon to stir in the sugar and vanilla. Leave to cool for a couple of minutes then stir in the beaten egg.

Sift the flour and cocoa onto the mixture then mix in. When thoroughly combined stir in the nuts. Transfer the mixture to the prepared pan and spread evenly.

Bake in the preheated oven for about 12 to 15 minutes or until just firm to the touch. Leave to cool then remove from the pan.

To finish: chop up the brownie into pieces roughly the size of your thumb nail. Transfer the ice cream to the fridge to soften (without letting it start to melt) then mix in the brownie pieces. Spoon the mixture into a freezerproof container and freeze until firm.

Serve with a pitcher of hot sauce. Choose from Butterscotch Fudge Sauce, Chocolate Fudge Sauce (see page 61) or Coffee Sauce (see page 62).

sauces

chocolate fudge sauce

A lovely thick and rich hot sauce that's not too sweet.

6 oz. good bittersweet chocolate

3 tablespoons unsalted butter

2 tablespoons golden syrup or light corn syrup

¾ cup light cream or half and half

Makes 4 to 6 servings

Break up the chocolate and put it in a small, heavy-based saucepan with the butter, syrup, and cream.

Set the saucepan over low heat and melt gently, stirring constantly. Continue stirring and heating until the mixture is almost at a boil. Pour the sauce into a warmed pitcher and serve immediately. The sauce will thicken as it cools but can be gently reheated.

Any leftover sauce can be covered and stored in the fridge for up to 2 days. Reheat gently before using.

butterscotch fudge sauce

A deliciously rich sauce. Good served with blondies.

6 tablespoons butter

1¼ cup firm-packed soft light brown sugar

2 tablespoons golden syrup or light corn syrup

½ cup heavy cream

Makes 6 servings

Put the butter, sugar, and syrup in a small, heavy-based saucepan. Melt gently over very low heat, stirring frequently, until the sugar dissolves completely (about 10 minutes).

When smooth and melted, stir in the cream then raise the heat and stir until the sauce is piping hot but not at a boil. Pour the sauce into a warmed pitcher and serve immediately.

Any leftover sauce can be covered and stored in the fridge for up to 3 days. Reheat gently before using.

creamy chocolate sauce

A simple yet rich sauce with no added sugar.

½ cup heavy cream

3 oz. good bittersweet chocolate, chopped

½ teaspoon real vanilla extract

Makes 4 to 6 servings

Pour the cream into a small, heavy-based saucepan and heat gently, stirring frequently. When the cream comes to a boil remove the saucepan from the heat and let cool for a minute. Stir in the chopped chocolate and vanilla and keep stirring until the sauce is smooth. Pour into a warmed pitcher and serve immediately.

The sauce will thicken as it cools but can be gently reheated.

Any leftover sauce can be stored, tightly covered, in the fridge for up to 2 days. Reheat very gently, stirring constantly, before using.

white chocolate sauce

Choose top-quality white chocolate flavored with real vanilla beans (not children's bars) for a good rich taste.

7 oz. good white chocolate

1 cup heavy cream

⅓ cup milk (not fat-free)

1 vanilla bean

Makes 4 to 6 servings

Break up the chocolate and put it in a heatproof bowl, set over a saucepan of steaming water.

Allow to melt gently, stirring frequently. Remove the bowl from the saucepan and leave to cool.

Put the cream and milk into a small, heavy-based saucepan. Split the vanilla bean lengthways (to expose the tiny seeds inside) and add to the saucepan. Heat, stirring constantly, until scalding hot but not quite at a boil.

Remove from the heat and let stand for 5 minutes. Remove the vanilla bean then pour the hot cream and milk onto the melted chocolate in a thin stream, whisking constantly, to make a smooth sauce. Pour into a warmed pitcher and serve immediately.

Any leftover sauce can be stored, tightly covered, in the fridge for up to 2 days. Reheat very gently, stirring constantly, before serving.

coffee sauce

Use good, well-flavored coffee but not espresso (or you can dilute espresso until it tastes like filter or cafétiere coffee.)

3½ oz. good bittersweet chocolate

4 tablespoons unsalted butter

½ cup good coffee

Makes 4 to 6 servings

Break up the chocolate and put it in a heatproof bowl. Add the butter and coffee then set the bowl over a saucepan of steaming water.

Allow to melt gently, stirring frequently, until very smooth. Remove the bowl from the saucepan and stir until glossy and slightly thickened. As the sauce cools it will become even thicker. Pour into a warmed pitcher and serve immediately.

Any leftover sauce can be stored, tightly covered, in the fridge for up to 2 days. Reheat very gently, stirring constantly, before serving.

index

conversion chart

Weights and measures have been rounded up or down slightly to make measuring easier.

Measuring butter:

A US stick of butter weighs 4 oz. which is approximately 115 g or 8 tablespoons. The recipes in this book require the following conversions:

American	Metric	Imperial
6 tbsp	85 g	3 oz.
7 tbsp	100 g	3½ oz.
1 stick	115 g	4 oz.

Volume equivalents:

American	Metric	Imperial
1 teaspoon	5 ml	
1 tablespoon	15 ml	
¼ cup	60 ml	2 fl.oz.
⅓ cup	75 ml	2½ fl.oz.
½ cup	125 ml	4 fl.oz.
⅔ cup	150 ml	5 fl.oz. (¼ pint)
¾ cup	175 ml	6 fl.oz.
1 cup	250 ml	8 fl.oz.

Weight equivalents:

Imperial	Metric
1 oz.	30 g
2 oz.	55 g
3 oz.	85 g
3½ oz.	100 g
4 oz.	115 g
5 oz.	140 g
6 oz.	175 g
8 oz. (½ lb.)	225 g
9 oz.	250 g
10 oz.	280 g
11½ oz.	325 g
12 oz.	350 g
13 oz.	375 g
14 oz.	400 g
15 oz.	425 g
16 oz. (1 lb.)	450 g

Measurements:

Inches	Cm
¼ inch	5 mm
½ inch	1 cm
¾ inch	1.5 cm
1 inch	2.5 cm
2 inches	5 cm
3 inches	7 cm
4 inches	10 cm
5 inches	12 cm
6 inches	15 cm
7 inches	18 cm
8 inches	20 cm
9 inches	23 cm
10 inches	25 cm
11 inches	28 cm
12 inches	30 cm

Oven temperatures:

150°C	(300°F)	Gas 2
170°C	(325°F)	Gas 3
180°C	(350°F)	Gas 4
190°C	(375°F)	Gas 5
200°C	(400°F)	Gas 6